CREATURE CRAFTS

ZOO ANIMALS

Annalees Lim

WAYLAND

CONTENTS

Welcome to the world of zoo animals!

Zoos are great places to discover new animals that you have never seen before. The next time you take a trip to the zoo, see if you can spot all of the animals that are in this book. In the meantime, this book will show you how to make them and tell you lots of fun facts about them, too!

Some of the projects use paint and craft glue. When using these, always cover surfaces with a piece of plastic or layers of old newspaper. Whenever you can, leave the project to dry before moving on to the next step. This avoids things getting stuck to each other or paint smudging.

So, do you have your craft tools at the ready? Then get set to make your crafty creatures and discover what makes each of them so special!

You can follow QR codes to watch videos of how some of the crafts are made!

LOOKOUT MEERKAT

In the wild, meerkats live in parts of southern Africa. You will often see lookout meerkats standing on their hind legs, keeping an eye out for any danger.

You will need:
Yoghurt drink bottle
Brown paper bag
Brown paper
A4 card
Glue stick
Googly eyes
Pencil
Double-sided tape
Sticky tape
Scissors
Brown felt tipped pen

1 Cover the yoghurt drink bottle in strips of double-sided tape. Peel off the back of the tape and stick on the brown paper bag.

2 Glue some brown paper onto the card.

3

Fold the paper-covered card in half and draw on a head, making sure that the nose touches the folded edge. Cut out the head and open it up.

4

Draw 2 arms, 2 legs and a tail onto the paper-covered card and cut them out.

5

Stick the arms, legs and tail to the bottle. Glue the googly eyes to the face and draw on the details with the brown felt tipped pen. Use sticky tape to fix the head to the bottle.

MEERKAT FACT
Young meerkats often help look after their newborn brothers and sisters.

TISSUE BOX ELEPHANT

Elephants are the largest animals that live on land. They can weigh up to 7,000 kilograms – that's about as much as four cars!

1

Wrap the tissue box neatly with grey paper, sticking it down with sticky tape.

2

Cut the 2 tubes in half and cover all 4 pieces in grey paper. Stick all the tubes to the bottom of the box with sticky tape.

3

Cut out a rectangle of grey card and curve it around the front of the box to make the head. Fix it to the box with sticky tape.

4

Cut out some ears, a trunk and a tail from grey card. Stick all of them to your elephant.

5

Draw 2 tusks and 4 sets of toes onto white paper. Cut them all out and stick them to your elephant. Draw on the eyes with the black marker pen.

ELEPHANT FACT
Did you know that elephants can swim very well? They use their trunk like a snorkel, so they can breathe when they are underwater!

EGG BOX CAMEL

You will need:
- Egg box
- Yellow pipe cleaners
- Yellow pom pom
- Yellow crêpe paper
- Sticky tape
- Scissors
- Black card
- Googly eyes
- Craft glue

Camels live in places with hot weather. They have one or two bulges on their backs, called humps. This crafty camel's hump is made out of an egg box!

1 Cover an egg box section with yellow crêpe paper. Tuck any excess crêpe paper inside the egg box section. Use sticky tape to hold in place.

2 Cut 2 pipe cleaners in half. Stick the 4 pieces inside the egg box section to form the legs. Bend each of the ends to make the feet. This should mean that your camel can stand on its own.

3

Bend the end of a pipe cleaner to form two ears. Stick the pipe cleaner to the front of the camel, using sticky tape.

4

Make a tail out of a small section of pipe cleaner. Stick it to the back of the camel. Stick the pom pom to the pipe cleaner that forms the neck and ears.

5

Glue googly eyes on the pom pom. Cut out a small triangle of black card to make the nose and glue it to the pom pom as well.

CAMEL FACT

People who live in the desert often ride camels. They also use camel milk for food.

FOAM MONKEY

You will need:
Brown, black and white foam
Craft glue
Stapler
Scissors

Monkeys often live in woodland areas. They are very good climbers, and use their arms, legs and tail to swing from tree to tree.

1

Cut brown foam into 4 strips that are the same size. Staple 2 into rings and staple one strip to each ring.

2

Staple both rings with their strips together, so that the rings form an '8'.

3

Cut out 4 short strips of brown foam. Bend each of them to form a loop and staple them to the ends of the long strips.

4

Cut out 2 brown foam circles that are big enough to cover the rings. Cut out 2 small circles and stick them to one of the larger circles. Stick the larger circles to the rings.

5

Use white foam to make your monkey's face, inner ears and belly. Use black foam to make 2 eyes, a nose, a mouth and a belly button. Glue these all in place.

MONKEY FACT
Monkeys are our closest living relative! They have hands that look like ours, with thumbs that help them to grip, eat food and groom.

STR ZEBRA

You will need:
- Double-sided tape
- Googly eyes
- Scissors
- White and black felt
- White card (optional)
- Ruler
- Craft glue

Zebras are covered in black and white stripes. Each zebra has a stripy pattern that is one of a kind. You can make your zebra's pattern unique, too!

1

Cut out a piece of white felt that is A5-sized. Stick at least 3 strips of double-sided tape onto the black felt. Cut into thin strips and stick these to your white felt.

2

Roll your striped felt into a tube and stick the edges together using double-sided tape. If your felt is not thick enough to hold its shape, stick it to some white card first.

3

Use the white and black felt to make a zebra head and legs, with hooves.

4

Glue all of the felt pieces together. Stick them to the body of your zebra using double-sided tape.

5

Stick googly eyes onto your zebra's face.

ZEBRA FACT

Did you know that zebras don't lie down to sleep? They snooze while they are standing!

TISSUE PAPER LION

You can tell a male lion from a female one because males have large manes. Make your lion have a big, bushy mane using lots of tissue paper.

You will need:
Two brown envelopes (size C6)
Orange tissue paper
Glue stick
Googly eyes
Black felt tipped pen
Scissors
Sticky tape

1

Fold the corners of one of the envelopes inwards. This will form your lion's face. Cut a small semi circle out of a short side of the other envelope.

2

Fold open the semi circle and cut it along the fold. Use the 2 semi circles to make your lion's ears. Stick them to either side of its head.

3

Cut rectangles out of the orange tissue. Fold them like a concertina. Stick them around the back of the folded envelope. Pull the ends apart to form the mane.

4

Draw the details of the face on using the black felt tipped pen.

LION FACT
Lions live in groups of 10-15 animals. These groups are called prides.

5

Stick the head and body of your lion together using the glue stick. Glue on googly eyes.

STRAW FLAMINGO

You will need:
Pink bendy drinking straws
Pink tissue paper
Pink, black and orange paper
Scissors
Glue stick
Sticky tape
Ruler
Googly eye

Flamingoes are large, pink birds that often stand on just one leg. Make your straw flamingo so that it balances on one leg, too!

1

Trim 2 straws so that there is the same amount of straw either side of their bendy parts. Insert one straw inside the other. This will form your flamingo's bent leg.

2

Bend the short part of a different straw to form the straight leg. Take another straw and cut it 6cm above the bend. Bend this too, to form your flamingo's neck.

16

3

Cut out a body shape and head shape from the pink paper. Stick the straws forming the legs to the body shape. Stick the straw forming the neck to the head shape.

4

Stick the body parts together. Cut out a beak shape from black paper and glue it to the head, together with a googly eye.

5

Cut out a circle of tissue paper and fold it like a concertina. This will form the wing. Stick this to your flamingo, along with some feet made from orange card.

FLAMINGO FACT

Did you know that flamingos are so pink because of the food they eat? When they eat different food, they turn almost white!

17

PRINTED PAPER LEMUR

You will need:
A4 white card
Sponge
Black and grey paint
Black and yellow paper
Glue stick
Scissors
Black felt tipped pen
Paint palette

Most of the world's lemurs live on an island by Africa, called Madagascar. You can have fun making your own ring-tailed lemur by printing with a sponge!

1

Use the sponge to colour half of your white card in grey. Only press the sponge down lightly, so that you create a patchy pattern.

2

Clean the sponge and use it to paint some black stripes onto the other half of your card. Leave the bottom third of this section white. Leave the card to dry.

3

On the grey side, use the black felt tipped pen to draw the body, arms and legs of your lemur.

4

On the other side of the card, draw a curly tail on the striped part and a head on the white part. Cut out all the shapes.

5

Cut out pieces from the grey card to form the top of the head and the tufts. Cut out 2 patches and a nose from black paper, and 2 eyes from yellow paper. Glue all the pieces together. Draw on the pupils with the black felt tipped pen.

LEMUR FACT

Lemurs love to be in the sun! They enjoy sitting in the sunshine, sometimes for whole afternoons.

PAPER PLATE SEA LION

You will need:
3 x paper plates
Blue, pink and purple paint
Black card
Googly eye
Scissors
Paint brush
Glue stick
Black felt tipped pen
Paint palette

Sea lions spend a lot of time in the water and are great swimmers. They can hold their breath for at least 10 minutes when they are underwater!

1

Paint 3 paper plates, one in blue, one in purple and one in pink. Leave them to dry.

2

Cut a curved shape out of the pink plate and stick it to the blue plate. This will form a rock for your sea lion.

3

Draw a sea lion body, fin and tail onto the purple plate. Cut out all the shapes.

4

Cut out a nose from a piece of black card. Stick this onto the head, along with a googly eye.

5

Glue all the pieces together onto the blue plate.

SEA LION FACT
Male sea lions are called bulls, females are called cows and baby sea lions are called pups.

PLASTIC POT TIGER

Tigers have orange coats with black stripes. Like the stripy pattern on a zebra, each tiger's coat is unique. Your tiger can have its very own special stripes!

1

Cover the yoghurt pot with orange card. If your pot has a label, you can remove it and use it as a template for the orange card.

2

Cut strips of black tape into triangles and stick them onto the side of the pot. These are your tiger's stripes.

3

Make 2 ears out of orange card. Stick them to the top of the pot.

4

Add the inside of the ears, a nose and a mouth. You can use either electrical tape or a black felt tipped pen for this. Use the glue stick to add googly eyes.

5

Tape some thin black stripes onto a piece of orange card and cut out 4 legs. Stick these to your tiger's body.

TIGER FACT

Did you know that tigers are great swimmers? They go for a dip to cool off when the weather is hot.

GLOSSARY

coat	an animal's fur
concertina	an instrument that makes a sound when its sack is squeezed and then pulled apart again; the sack has many folds
groom	when an animal cleans its own or another animal's fur
hind legs	an animal's back legs
mane	long hair around a male lion's face
template	a shape that is used as a guide to cut out something
trunk	the nose of an elephant; it is long and shaped a bit like a hose
unique	when something is one of a kind, not like anything else

INDEX

First published in Great Britain in 2015 by Wayland

Copyright © Wayland, 2015

Wayland, an imprint of Hachette Children's Group
Part of Hodder and Stoughton

Carmelite House
50 Victoria Embankment
London, EC4Y 0DZ

All rights reserved.

An Hachette UK Company
www.hachette.co.uk www.hachettechildrens.co.uk

Series editor: Julia Adams
Craft photography: Simon Pask, N1 Studios
Additional images: Shutterstock

Dewey classification: 745.5-dc23
ISBN: 9780750295444
ebook ISBN: 9780750296922

Printed in China

The QR codes included in this book were valid at the time of going to press. However, because of the nature of the Internet, it is possible that addresses may have changed, or sites may have changed or closed down, since publication.

MIX
Paper from responsible sources
FSC® C104740
FSC www.fsc.org

Get your paws on all the books in the Creature Crafts series!

978 0 7502 8448 6

978 0 7502 8447 9

978 0 7502 9543 7

978 0 7502 8446 2

978 0 7502 8449 3

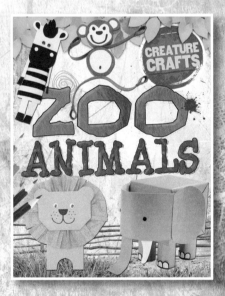

978 0 7502 9544 4